READ & RESPOND

Bringing the best books to life in the classroom

Activities based on Alice's Adventures in Wonderland

By Lewis Carroll

ALICE'S
ADVENTURES IN
WONDERLAND

Lewis Carroll

FOR AGES 7–11

Scholastic Education, an imprint of Scholastic Ltd
Book End, Range Road, Witney, Oxfordshire, OX29 0YD
Registered office: Westfield Road, Southam, Warwickshire CV47 0RA

Printed and bound by Ashford Colour Press
© 2017 Scholastic Ltd
1 2 3 4 5 6 7 8 9   7 8 9 0 1 2 3 4 5 6

British Library Cataloguing-in-Publication Data
A catalogue record for this book is available from the British Library.
ISBN 978-1407-17616-1

Authors Sally Burt and Debbie Ridgard
Editorial team Audrey Stokes, Vicki Yates, Julia Roberts, Suzanne Adams
Series designers Neil Salt and Alice Duggan
Designer Alice Duggan
Illustrator Kate Sheppard/Beehive Illustration

Acknowledgements
The publishers gratefully acknowledge permission to reproduce the following copyright material:
Scholastic Children's Books for permission to use the cover from Alice's Adventures in Wonderland written by Lewis Carroll (Scholastic Children's Books, 2014).
Reproduced with permission of Scholastic Children's Books. All rights reserved.

Photographs
page 8: Lewis Carroll, Shutterstock.

Every effort has been made to trace copyright holders for the works reproduced in this book, and the publishers apologise for any inadvertent omissions.

CONTENTS

How to use Read & Respond in your classroom...

Read & Respond provides teaching ideas related to a specific well-loved children's book. Each Read & Respond book is divided into the following sections:

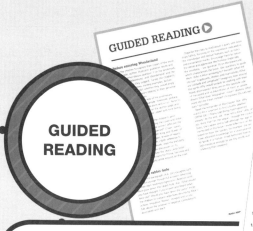

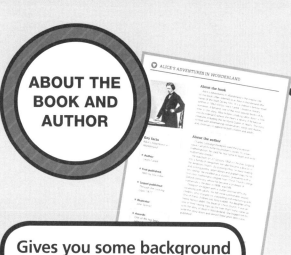

ABOUT THE BOOK AND AUTHOR

Gives you some background information about the book and the author.

GUIDED READING

Breaks the book down into sections and gives notes for using it with guided reading groups. A bookmark has been provided on page 12 containing comprehension questions. The children can be directed to refer to these as they read.

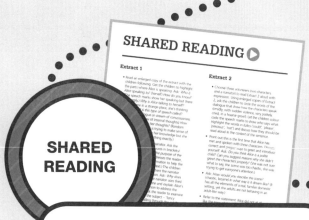

SHARED READING

Provides extracts from the children's book with associated notes for focused work. There is also one non-fiction extract that relates to the children's book.

GRAMMAR, PUNCTUATION & SPELLING

Provides word-level work related to the children's book so you can teach grammar, punctuation and spelling in context.

PLOT, CHARACTER & SETTING

Contains activity ideas focused on the plot, characters and the setting of the story.

GET WRITING

Provides writing activities related to the children's book. These activities may be based directly on the children's book or be broadly based on the themes and concepts of the story.

TALK ABOUT IT

Has speaking and listening activities related to the children's book. These activities may be based directly on the children's book or be broadly based on the themes and concepts of the story.

ASSESSMENT

Contains short activities that will help you assess whether the children have understood concepts and curriculum objectives. They are designed to be informal activities to feed into your planning.

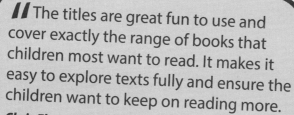

" The titles are great fun to use and cover exactly the range of books that children most want to read. It makes it easy to explore texts fully and ensure the children want to keep on reading more. "

Chris Flanagan, Year 5 Teacher,
St Thomas of Canterbury
Primary School

Activities

The activities follow the same format:

- **Objective:** the objective for the lesson. It will be based upon a curriculum objective, but will often be more specific to the focus being covered.

- **What you need:** a list of resources you need to teach the lesson, including printable pages.

- **What to do:** the activity notes.

- **Differentiation:** this is provided where specific and useful differentiation advice can be given to support and/or extend the learning in the activity. Differentiation by providing additional adult support has not been included as this will be at a teacher's discretion based upon specific children's needs and ability, as well as the availability of support.

The activities are numbered for reference within each section and should move through the text sequentially – so you can use the lesson while you are reading the book. Once you have read the book, most of the activities can be used in any order you wish.

Section	Activity	Curriculum objectives
Guided reading		Comprehension: To maintain positive attitudes to reading and understanding of what they read.
Shared reading	1	Comprehension: To draw inferences such as inferring characters' feelings, thoughts and motives from their actions.
	2	Comprehension: To identify how language, structure and presentation contribute to meaning.
	3	Comprehension: To check that the book makes sense, discuss their understanding and explore words in context.
	4	Comprehension: To read and discuss an increasingly wide range of...non-fiction and reference books.
Grammar, punctuation & spelling	1	Vocabulary, grammar and punctuation: To use passive verbs to affect the presentation of information in a sentence.
	2	Transcription: To distinguish between homophones and other easily confused words.
	3	Transcription: To spell some words with 'silent' letters.
	4	Vocabulary, grammar and punctuation: To use the perfect form of verbs to mark relationships of time.
	5	Vocabulary, grammar and punctuation: To use expanded noun phrases.
	6	Vocabulary, grammar and punctuation: To punctuate bullet points consistently.
Plot, character & setting	1	Comprehension: To increase familiarity with a wide range of books, including myths, legends and traditional stories, modern fiction, fiction from our literary heritage, and books from other cultures and traditions.
	2	Comprehension: To draw inference...and justify inference with evidence.
	3	Comprehension: To identify and discuss themes.
	4	Comprehension: To ask questions to improve their understanding.
	5	Comprehension: To distinguish between statements of fact and opinion.
	6	Comprehension: To identify how language and presentation contribute to meaning.
	7	Comprehension: To identify how...structure...contributes to meaning..
	8	Comprehension: To distinguish between fact and opinion; to provide justifications for their views.

Section	Activity	Curriculum objectives
Talk about it	1	Spoken language: To speak audibly and fluently.
	2	Comprehension: To prepare poems to read aloud and perform.
	3	Spoken language: To gain, maintain and monitor the interest of the listener(s).
	4	Spoken language: To participate in...and debates.
	5	Spoken language: To participate in...performances.
	6	Spoken language: To consider and evaluate different viewpoints.
Get writing	1	Composition: To propose changes to vocabulary...and clarify meaning.
	2	Composition: To identify the purpose of the writing, selecting the appropriate form.
	3	Composition: To describe characters...integrating dialogue to convey character.
	4	Composition: To consider how authors have developed characters and settings in writing narratives; to proofread for spelling and punctuation errors.
	5	Composition: To use organisational and presentational devices to structure text and guide the reader.
	6	Composition: To identify the audience for and purpose of the writing, selecting appropriate form, using other similar writing as models.
Assessment	1	Comprehension: To understand what they read by drawing inferences; to check that the book makes sense to them.
	2	Spoken language: To participate actively in collaborative conversations, staying on topic and initiating and responding to comments.
	3	Transcription: To use a dictionary to check spelling and meaning of words.
	4	Comprehension: To discuss and evaluate how authors use language, including figurative language.
	5	Composition: To use further organisational and presentational devices to structure text and to guide the reader.
	6	Composition: To write narratives, considering how authors have developed characters and settings; to ensure the consistent and correct use of tense throughout a piece of writing.

About the book

Alice's Adventures in Wonderland is the original title of the book often referred to as Alice in Wonderland (the name of the Walt Disney film). It is a children's fantasy novel written in 1862–63 by Lewis Carroll. Classed as literary nonsense, it became one of the most popular books of its time. In the story, Alice follows a talking rabbit down a hole into Wonderland where she meets a variety of fantastical creatures including the terrifying Queen of Hearts. The story is filled with entertaining conversations, songs and rhymes, and continues to appeal to both children and adults.

About the author

Charles Lutwidge Dodgson used the pseudonym Lewis Carroll to write his children's novels. As a keen mathematician, he used his real name to teach and write mathematics books.

He was born on 27 January 1832 in Cheshire, England, into a family of clergymen. He later became a deacon in the Anglican Church. As a young child, he loved reading and writing poetry, short stories and puppet plays for his ten siblings. He excelled as a student, graduating with a first-class mathematics degree from Christ Church College, Oxford University, where he became a professor of mathematics. He died in 1898, aged 66.

Dodgson struggled with a stutter and had difficulty socialising with adults. He felt more comfortable around children, who enjoyed his storytelling and entertaining skills. One of these children was Alice Liddell, the daughter of his friend Henry Liddell, the Dean of Christ Church. It was on one of their rowing trips up the river that Charles came up with the story of Alice in Wonderland. She begged him to write the story down and almost three years later it was published.

About the illustrator

Alice in Wonderland was illustrated by John Tenniel, who was born in London in 1820 and died there at the age of 94. He was the chief political cartoonist for Punch magazine for over 50 years. He produced over 2000 political cartoons, but remains most famous for the 92 illustrations he did for the Alice books. Lewis Carroll approached him to do the illustrations because he liked his style – a mixture of real and grotesque, which Carroll believed suited the story.

GUIDED READING ▶

Before entering Wonderland

Invite the children to explore their copies of the book – cover, title, author, illustrator, publisher, blurb and so on. Together discuss question 1 on the bookmark, focusing on 'Adventures' and 'Wonderland' and the different genres they suggest. Survey the children's own preferred genres, inviting examples, before asking them to predict whether they would enjoy this novel, giving reasons relating to their personal reading and preferences.

Together discuss the role of the preliminary features of books, for example: foreword, preface, prologue, quotation, dedication and so on. Refer to the information provided on the author page and explain the link to the three Liddell girls (one being Alice).

Ascertain the extent of the children's prior knowledge of the story using the cover and initial illustration. Ask: *What is the scene? Who are the characters? What has happened?* (Cover: varies; illustration: court scene with King and Queen of Hearts and the White Rabbit; Knave of Hearts is accused of stealing tarts.) With reference to question 6 on the bookmark, read the prefatory poem and initiate a class discussion on its purpose – it explains how the story came to be written – as entertainment for Prima, Secunda and Tertia (the Liddell girls) while rowing on the river.

Down the rabbit-hole

Read the first paragraph. Ask: *Do you agree with Alice?* (Encourage thoughtful answers reflecting on their own reading progression.) Read on until Alice goes down the rabbit-hole. Ask: *What would you have thought if you'd seen and heard what Alice did? Would you have done the same?* Invite the children to suggest adjectives describing Alice's actions (impulsive, foolish, intrepid and so on). Talk about the positive or negative connotations associated with each.

Organise the class to read aloud in pairs until Alice stops falling, focusing on the expression indicated in the monologue and textual features such as italics and exclamation marks. Encourage them to notice the detail and appreciate the humour (especially the wordplay – see question 10 on the bookmark) which characterises the book. Use questions to guide them: *Who is Alice speaking to?* (herself) *What did she see?* (cupboards, shelves and marmalade) *What are Latitude and Longitude?* (imaginary lines around the earth) *Why would people be walking with their heads downwards?* (they are on the opposite side of the world and so Alice thinks of them as upside down) *What does 'Antipathies' mean?* (dislikes) *What word did she mean instead?* (Antipodes) *Do cats eat bats?* (possibly)

Read the remainder of the chapter. Ask: *Why wasn't Alice surprised to find a bottle labelled 'DRINK ME'?* (Many odd things had happened already.) At the end, ask: *How old is Alice? Why do you think that?* (In the sequel, *Through the Looking-Glass*, she's seven and a half although her age isn't mentioned in this book.) Invite reflections on Alice based on how she speaks, for example, she seems to have advanced knowledge for a seven-year-old and to speak in a mature, if old-fashioned manner, while still immature enough to use big words without knowing their meaning.

Size matters

Ask: *What did Alice want in Chapter 1?* (to enter the garden) *Why couldn't she get there?* (too big, then couldn't reach the key). Invite the children to read to the end of Chapter 4 in pairs, discussing questions 2 and 9 on the bookmark. Hold a plenary and invite volunteers to summarise the chapters and share events they found particularly absurd. Remind them to note and look up unfamiliar words, for example, 'kid gloves', 'carrier', 'fender', 'hearthrug' or 'hookah'.

Ask: *How did Alice offend the mouse and the birds?* (mentioned Dinah was an avid mouse/bird eater) *Could she have been more sensitive?* (yes) End by asking: *After encountering the puppy, why does Alice think she should eat something?* (to grow the right size again)

A caterpillar, a Duchess, a cat and a tea party

Choose three volunteers to read Chapter 5 with you. One child should be the caterpillar, one Alice, one the pigeon and you should be the narrator. Remind the children that Alice has questioned her identity since entering the rabbit-hole and ask: *How would you reply to the caterpillar's first question?* Encourage reflective answers. Ask: *Why does Alice believe she's changed? Has she?* (Her size keeps changing and she can't remember things properly; yes and no.) Together, discuss question 16 on the bookmark in relation to the caterpillar. He looks old and wise but treats Alice disdainfully despite being ultimately helpful. Ask, again in relation to question 16: *Why did the pigeon think Alice was a serpent?* Invite a general discussion on classification – of animals, plants and so on, focusing on how we choose to define and differentiate one thing or person from another.

Ask the children to read Chapters 6 and 7 in groups while considering questions 4, 9, 16 and 17 from the bookmark. Invite a group spokesperson to report their findings. Ask: *Why does the Cheshire-Cat tell Alice she is mad? Is he right?* (because she's in Wonderland; accept thoughtful answers)

Enter the Queen of Hearts

Read Chapter 8 aloud as a class or in groups. Encourage the children to skim first and then to act or read it out. Afterwards refer to question 9 on the bookmark. List their findings on the board before voting on the favourite. Ask the children to read to the end of Chapter 11. Explain that 'mock turtle soup' is a real recipe although not made of turtles – the Mock Turtle's very existence therefore sets the scene for his absurd story laden with word play. Bring the class together to share aspects they particularly enjoyed. At the end, ask: *What starts to happen to Alice in court? What does this signify?* (She starts to grow; she feels more powerful and in control as she grows in stature.) Encourage the children to consider question 7 on the bookmark as you read the final chapter to the class. Ask: *Why is Alice so angry? What does she do?* (She is increasingly annoyed by the trial's absurd chaos and finally calls them what they are – a pack of cards.) Invite the children's opinions on the ending – usually it's not encouraged to 'wake up and find it was all a dream' at the end of a story. Together discuss question 5 on the bookmark. There is no clear answer. Although Alice seems to learn a few things like being more sensitive to 'people' she encounters, the way she skips off calling it a 'wonderful dream' suggests that is all it was to her.

Structure

After reading the book, discuss question 7 on the bookmark. The book contains standard features like illustrations, characters and chapters that flow logically from one to the next, but the plot is less clear or logical. Discuss question 15 on the bookmark, inviting suggestions backed by evidence. Alice is clearly the protagonist (the main character). The Queen of Hearts is usually considered the primary antagonist (the character who opposes or fights against the main character) yet she doesn't stand in opposition to Alice. She is an illogical, irascible character who must just be managed. The Knave of Hearts' trial is often viewed as the climax, and while it is a dramatic scene, it doesn't relate to Alice 'solving a problem' or 'resolving a conflict'. In some ways, Alice's adventures are more a parody of a traditional hero journey where the hero is called, enters a different world and is tested while being guided by a mentor. Ask: *Is Alice a hero? Was she 'called'? What are her challenges? Does she face a final test? Does she return changed?* (not really; no; many: size, lack of logic, unclear rules; no evidence)

Style

Having been written over 150 years ago, the language is that of Victorian England, although the effect is offset by the nonsense and invention. Ask the children to reflect on bookmark question 13; for example, invite children to suggest adjectives describing how Alice talks to herself and how the different characters speak, and try out speaking as they do. Maintain two class vocabulary lists, one for unfamiliar words and the other for invented words, and remind the children to keep a dictionary handy.

The punctuation differs slightly from modern usage: punctuation has changed over time as well as language; for example, exclamation marks mid-sentence, liberal use of colons and semicolons, and above all, very long sentences. Refer to question 12 on the bookmark and encourage the children to find examples of the author's use of punctuation, italics and other textual features for emphasis and expression.

The book has had various illustrators over the years, but the initial illustrations were made iconic by the Walt Disney animated film. Together discuss question 6 on the bookmark, focusing on the exceptional detail in the black-and-white line drawings.

Skim the story together and review question 11 on the bookmark. Ask: *Are rhymes and songs important to the plot? Why does the author include them?* (no; to increase the nonsense and enjoyment) Find out the class's favourite rhyme or song.

Setting

Apart from beginning and ending on a riverbank, the action all happens in Wonderland. Ask the children to discuss bookmark question 18. Remind them of the story's Victorian context and ask: *How would Wonderland have differed from Alice's world?* Encourage them to appreciate how it is described in a way that is characteristic of dreams – mirroring the world in a lopsided or ludicrous fashion, for example the croquet game or the court scene.

Characters

After reading the book, ask: *Apart from Alice, who are the story's main characters? Why?* Note the medley of characters that help or hinder Alice. Discuss questions 3 and 5 on the bookmark, then ask the children to focus on question 16 and choose a character to share with the class.

Themes

After reading, together reflect on question 8 on the bookmark. The book has many underlying themes: childhood versus adulthood; identity; the nature of society and the adult world; dreams versus reality; as well as words, meaning and nonsense. In Wonderland, Alice questions everything, including language: misunderstanding and humour are created because characters often don't use the expected dictionary meanings of words, appearing to invent their own meanings instead.

Alice's adventures can also be seen as her way of dealing with the challenges of growing up in a world where adults often act in a confusing and illogical way. The story mirrors the real and unfamiliar changes a child has to deal with as the body grows and develops. As Alice's body changes in unexpected ways, she questions not just who she is but also identity in general, all while trying to comprehend the seemingly random behaviour and responses of the characters she encounters.

Use your discretion about which themes to discuss and in what depth. While it is an opportunity to broach a range of PSHE topics and cross-curricular topics, on first reading you may not want to detract from their appreciation of Alice's imagination and the nonsense created by wordplay and inverted logic, especially as the story was intended to entertain rather than make serious observations.

Alice's Adventures in Wonderland
by Lewis Carroll

Focus on...
Meaning

1. What words in the title help you decide what genre of book this is? Does the rest of the cover support your idea?

2. What was the effect of Alice's change in size?

3. Why does Alice find many of the characters frustrating or rude?

4. What kind of character is the Cheshire-Cat?

5. Do you think Alice learned anything during her time in Wonderland?

Focus on...
Organisation

6. What did the author include before Chapter 1? Why do you think he did this?

7. How does the story follow or not follow traditional story structure?

8. What important themes run through the story?

Alice's Adventures in Wonderland
by Lewis Carroll

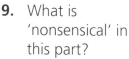

Focus on...
Language and features

9. What is 'nonsensical' in this part?

10. How is wordplay used in this chapter? Give examples.

11. What is the role of the poems, songs and rhymes in Wonderland?

12. How does the author use punctuation, italics and layout for effect?

13. Describe the language and style of the writing.

Focus on...
Purpose, viewpoints and effects

14. Describe the style of the illustrations. Do they help visualise the scenes?

15. Who are the main antagonists in the story? Why?

16. How do the characters' appearances and dialogue reflect their personalities?

17. What makes Alice question who she is and everything she knows?

18. Identify clues that show Wonderland is a dream world.

SHARED READING ▶

Extract 1

- Read an enlarged copy of the extract with the children following. Get the children to highlight the parts where Alice is speaking. Ask: *Who is Alice speaking to?* (herself) *How do you know?* (The speech marks show her speaking but there is no reply.) *Why is Alice talking to herself?* (She is alone in a strange place, she's thinking aloud.) *What is this type of speech called?* (internal monologue or stream of consciousness – showing the flow of internal thoughts) *How would you describe her thoughts?* (Random and dream-like. Alice is trying to make sense of her situation and apply her knowledge but she cannot remember everything exactly.)

- Consider the role of the narrator. Ask the children to highlight the words in brackets/parenthesis. Ask: *What is the purpose of the brackets?* (The narrator addresses the reader, providing background information to help the reader understand the context.) The children should identify the parts where the narrator uses third and second person. Ask: *Why does the narrator use both?* (The narrator uses third person to describe the scene and explain Alice's thoughts and second person to address the reader personally and ask the reader to examine his or her thoughts on the subject – 'fancy *curtseying* as you're falling through the air! Do you think you could manage it?')

- Circle all the 'grand' words Alice uses ('Latitude', 'Longitude', 'Antipathies', 'ignorant'). Explain the humour in Alice's use of the word 'Antipathies' (Alice meant to use the word 'Antipodes' which means on the opposite side of the earth, ie Australia and New Zealand. Instead, she used the word 'antipathies' meaning a deep dislike.)

Extract 2

- Choose three volunteers (two characters and a narrator) to read Extract 2 aloud with expression. Using enlarged copies of Extract 2, ask the children to circle the words of the dialogue that show how the characters speak (timidly, with sudden violence, very politely, cried, in a hoarse growl). Let the children colour code the speech marks to show who says what. Highlight the words in italics (*'could', 'please', 'precious', 'not'*) and discuss how they should be read aloud in the context of the sentence.

- Point out this is the first time that Alice has met and spoken with these characters. Discuss correct and proper ways to greet and introduce yourself. Ask: *Do you think Alice is a polite child? Can you suggest reasons why she didn't greet the characters properly?* (She was not sure what to say, the scene was too chaotic, she was trying to get everyone's attention.)

- Ask: *How would you describe the scene?* (chaotic, bizarre) *In what way is it dream-like?* (It has all the elements of a real, familiar domestic setting, yet the adults are not behaving in an adult-like way.)

- Refer to the statement 'Alice did not at all like the tone of this remark'. Ask: *What is the tone of the Duchess's remark, 'You don't know much,...and that's a fact'?* (insulting, condescending, rude) Suggest reasons why Alice took the remark personally. (The Duchess insulted her intelligence.) *How would you describe Alice's tone in the conversation?* (polite at first and later desperate and pleading)

- Dialogue gives insight into the characters. Ask: *How would you describe the Duchess?* (rude, cruel, doesn't know much herself – uses words and expressions incorrectly, moralistic)

Extract 3

- This extract is the start of the story's climax. Alice finally meets the Queen of Hearts. Read an enlarged copy with the class. Ask: *What is Alice's first impression?* (She is impressed but unsure whether she should lie down, bow or watch.) *Why did she decide not to lie down as the procession passed and what does this tell you about Alice?* (She wanted to see everything, she's inquisitive and independent, she's not easily intimidated.)

- Ask: *What is a procession?* (a group of people moving or marching in order, usually at a ceremony) *In what order did everyone appear?* (ten soldiers, ten courtiers, the royal children, the guests – mostly Kings and Queens and the White Rabbit, the Knave of Hearts, the King and Queen of Hearts) Encourage the children to locate words in the text that indicate the order of the procession ('first' 'next', 'after these', 'next', 'then followed', 'last of all'…). *What is strange about this procession?* (They're all cards except the White Rabbit.)

- Consider the use of speech marks. Let the children identify and highlight which speech marks show dialogue and which speech marks show Alice's thoughts. Ask: *Why does the author show Alice's thoughts in speech marks?* (To show Alice talking to herself.)

- Ask the children to find clues in the text that describe or imply how Alice felt before and after meeting the Queen. (At first, Alice was excited and 'eager to see the Queen'. Telling herself 'I needn't be afraid of them!' implies she was somewhat fearful in the Queen's presence at first, but then her bold responses show her becoming more defiant.

Extract 4

- Using an enlarged copy of Extract 4, ask the children to skim over it. Refer to the title and ask: *Is the text fiction or non-fiction? How can you tell?* (non-fiction; it has a heading and provides factual information about Victorian times) *What do you notice about the style of the language and the layout?* (The language is formal and precise, with no dialogue or detailed descriptions. The layout shows paragraphs that divide the text into sections.)

- Consider the paragraphs. Ask: *What is the main topic of each paragraph?* (First paragraph: introduction to childhood in the Victorian era; second paragraph: the lives of wealthy children; third paragraph: the lives of poor children; fourth paragraph: schools and classrooms; fifth paragraph: teachers and punishment.)

- Focus on the punctuation. Ask: *What are inverted commas used for?* (to indicate a quote or well-known expression) *What is the purpose of the comma in the third paragraph?* (to separate a list) *Find another example of this in the text.* (reading, writing) *What is the purpose of the comma in the first paragraph?* (separates two clauses) *What is the purpose of the colon in the first paragraph?* (to introduce a related thought or explanation) *Which words in the text are hyphenated and why?* ('well-dressed', 'well-fed', 'well-educated' are linked to form compound adjectives)

- Ask the children to compare the life of a wealthy Victorian child to that of a poor Victorian child. Ask: *Would you describe Alice as a wealthy or poor Victorian child? How can you tell?* (She was from a wealthy family because she was well-dressed and well-educated, and didn't have to work.)

Extract 1

Down, down, down. Would the fall *never* come to an end? "I wonder how many miles I've fallen by this time?" she said aloud. "I must be getting somewhere near the centre of the earth. Let me see: that would be four thousand miles down. I think – "(for, you see, Alice had learnt several things of this sort in her lessons in the schoolroom, and though this was not a very good opportunity for showing off her knowledge, as there was no one to listen to her, still it was good practice to say it over) "–yes, that's about the right distance – but then I wonder what Latitude or Longitude I've got to?" (Alice had no idea what Latitude was, or Longitude either, but thought they were nice grand words to say.)

Presently she began again. "I wonder if I shall fall right *through* the earth! How funny it'll seem to come out among the people that walk with their heads downwards! The Antipathies, I think –" (she was rather glad there *was* no one listening, this time, as it didn't sound at all the right word) "– but I shall have to ask them what the name of the country is, you know. Please, Ma'am, is this New Zealand or Australia?" (and she tried to curtsey as she spoke – fancy *curtseying* as you're falling through the air! Do you think you could manage it?) "And what an ignorant little girl she'll think me! No, it'll never do to ask: perhaps I shall see it written up somewhere."

Down, down, down. There was nothing else to do, so Alice soon began talking again.

Extract 2

"Please would you tell me," said Alice a little timidly, for she was not quite sure whether it was good manners for her to speak first, "why your cat grins like that?"

"It's a Cheshire-Cat," said the Duchess, "and that's why. Pig!"

She said the last word with such sudden violence that Alice quite jumped; but she saw in another moment that it was addressed to the baby, and not to her, so she took courage, and went on again:

"I didn't know that Cheshire-Cats always grinned; in fact, I didn't know that cats *could* grin."

"They all can," said the Duchess; "and most of 'em do."

"I don't know of any that do," Alice said very politely, feeling quite pleased to have got into a conversation.

"You don't know much," said the Duchess; "and that's a fact."

Alice did not at all like the tone of this remark, and thought it would be as well to introduce some other subject of conversation. While she was trying to fix on one, the cook took the cauldron of soup off the fire, and at once set to work throwing everything within her reach at the Duchess and the baby – the fire-irons came first; then followed a shower of saucepans, plates, and dishes. The Duchess took no notice of them even when they hit her; and the baby was howling so much already, that it was quite impossible to say whether the blows hurt it or not.

"Oh, *please* mind what you're doing," cried Alice, jumping up and down in an agony of terror. "Oh, there goes his *precious* nose!" as an unusually large saucepan flew close by it, and very nearly carried it off.

"If everybody minded their own business," the Duchess said in a hoarse growl, "the world would go round a deal faster than it does."

"Which would *not* be an advantage," said Alice, who felt very glad to get an opportunity of showing off a little of her knowledge. "Just think what work it would make with the day and night! You see the earth takes twenty-four hours to turn round on its axis—"

"Talking of axes," said the Duchess, "chop off her head."

Extract 3

There was a sound of many footsteps, and Alice looked round, eager to see the Queen.

First came ten soldiers carrying clubs; these were all shaped like the three gardeners, oblong and flat, with their hands and feet at the corners: next the ten courtiers; these were ornamented all over with diamonds, and walked two and two, as the soldiers did. After these came the royal children; there were ten of them, and the little dears came jumping merrily along hand in hand, in couples; they were all ornamented with hearts. Next came the guests, mostly Kings and Queens, and among them Alice recognized the White Rabbit: it was talking in a hurried, nervous manner, smiling at everything that was said, and went by without noticing her. Then followed the Knave of Hearts, carrying the King's crown on a crimson velvet cushion; and last of all this grand procession, came THE KING AND QUEEN OF HEARTS.

Alice was rather doubtful whether she ought not to lie down on her face like the three gardeners, but she could not remember ever having heard of such a rule at processions; "and besides, what would be the use of a procession," thought she, "if people had to lie down upon their faces, so that they couldn't see it?" So she stood still where she was, and waited.

When the procession came opposite to Alice, they all stopped and looked at her, and the Queen said severely, "Who is this?" She said it to the Knave of Hearts, who only bowed and smiled in reply.

"Idiot!" said the Queen, tossing her head impatiently; and turning to Alice, she went on, "What's your name, child?"

"My name is Alice, so please your Majesty," said Alice very politely; but she added, to herself, "Why, they're only a pack of cards, after all. I needn't be afraid of them!"

Extract 4

Children in Victorian times (1830–1900)

The story of Alice is set in the Victorian era when children 'were to be seen and not heard'. Childhood was a serious time: those who survived birth and infancy were at risk of dying from a deadly disease like smallpox or diphtheria. Stories generally had serious morals and children's literature was intended to teach and warn, not to entertain.

Wealthy children were well-dressed, well-fed and well-educated, usually at home, until the age of ten. Boys went on to attend public schools while girls continued their education at home. Children were taught to be proper and polite and had little contact with their parents. They were often bored and confined to their homes.

Children from poor families started working from as early as five years old. Jobs included factory work, selling flowers or fruit at the market, doing washing and housework and sweeping the streets. It was not unusual for an older brother or sister to walk their young sibling to work each day.

In 1870, Queen Victoria passed a law that made it compulsory for children to attend school up to the age of ten years. The Victorian classroom looked quite different from classrooms today. Classes had up to seventy children and were varied in ages and grades. The walls were bare and windows were placed high up so that children could not look outside. There was little creativity used to teach 'the three Rs' – reading, writing and arithmetic. Most lessons involved the teacher writing on the board and the children had to copy it down.

Teachers were generally very strict and often cruel. Children who were not quick enough or struggling had to stand on a chair or sit in the corner as punishment. Children who missed school or who were lazy were beaten with a stick and no one was allowed to write using their left hand.

GRAMMAR, PUNCTUATION & SPELLING ▶

1. Active or passive

Objective
To use the passive voice to change the effect of a sentence.

What you need
Copies of *Alice's Adventures in Wonderland*, photocopiable page 22 'Active or passive?'

What to do

• Write on the board 'The Knave of Hearts stole the tarts.' Revise subject and object by asking a volunteer to underline the subject and circle the object. Remind children that sentences with the subject doing the action are known as active (voice not tense). Invite the class to invent their own active sentences.

• Write the same sentence as above, showing how to form the passive voice using the verb 'to be' and the past participle: 'The tarts were stolen by the Knave of Hearts.' Ask: *How is the effect of this sentence different to the active one?* (The tarts have action done to them <u>by</u> an agent – the Knave.) Emphasise that although English is generally an active language (subject-verb-object word order), the passive is used for effect; for example, to hide the agent; *the tarts were stolen*; if the agent is unimportant: *tarts are baked on Tuesdays*; or to change focus – to make the tarts the focus rather than the Knave.

• Open photocopiable page 22 'Active or passive?' and discuss the different effects of the sentences before children complete the activities independently.

Differentiation
Support: Before working in pairs, help children to find the verbs in each sentence.

Extension: Ask children to find passive sentences in other chapters and discuss why the passive voice has been used in each one.

2. Check that word

Objective
To enjoy wordplay with homophones and other easily confused words.

What you need
Copies of *Alice's Adventures in Wonderland*, dictionaries, recipe for mock turtle soup.

Cross-curricular link
History

What to do

• Recap events in Chapter 9. Display a mock turtle soup recipe (available on the Internet). Explain it was a soup in Victorian times made as a cheap alternative to green turtle soup. Ask: *What is a Mock Turtle?* (what mock turtle soup is made from according to the Mock Turtle) *Do mock turtles exist?* (Ask for ideas backed by reasons.)

• Write on the board: 'mean', 'check', 'train', 'watch'. Invite volunteers to give the word classes and meanings for each. Using the multiple meanings as a teaching aid, discuss the difference between homonyms (spelled and sound the same but different meaning), homophones (sound the same but different spelling and meaning), homographs (spelled the same but different sound and meaning) and generally easily confused words (sound and spelling), giving examples of each.

• Organise the class into groups of four to re-read the Mock Turtle's story: narrator, Alice, Gryphon and Mock Turtle. Groups should identify examples of wordplay in the story and discuss the humour in each. Invite groups to share their examples, identifying the form of wordplay used.

Differentiation
Support: Place less confident children in mixed-ability groups.

Extension: Encourage children to look for more wordplay in earlier chapters.

3. Silent-letter croquet

Objective
To spell some words with 'silent' letters.

What you need
Photocopiable page 23 'Silent-letter croquet', counters, dice, notebooks.

What to do

- Begin by asking: *Who stole the tarts?* (Knave of Hearts) *What's the silent letter?* (k) Invite the children to give other examples of words with a silent k and compile a list on the board ('knot', 'know', 'knight', 'knuckle' and so on). Discuss whether any of the words have homophones if you take away the silent letter (for example, 'night', 'nave', 'new', 'nit', 'not') or whether the sound changes (for example, 'now').

- Ask volunteers for words containing other silent letters and group them on the board, underlining the silent letters. Remind the children that the silent letter can be at the beginning, in the middle or at the end of a word, prompting them with examples of your own, if necessary. Common silent letters include p ('pneumonia', 'receipt'), b ('comb', 'doubt'), w ('write', 'sword'), g ('sign', 'gnome'), n ('solemn', 'autumn'), t ('bristle', 'fasten'), u ('biscuit', 'built'), h ('character', 'school').

- Organise the class into groups of two or three to play a slient-letter game using photocopiable page 23 'Silent-letter croquet' as the board. Explain that they should use their notebooks to write the words and the other players can check the spelling using a dictionary.

Differentiation
Support: Monitor groups of children requiring extra support, joining in as appropriate.

Extension: Ask the children to gather everyone's word lists to make a giant wall poster of silent letter word groups for the classroom.

4. Perfect tenses

Objective
To use the perfect form of verbs to mark relationships of time.

What you need
Copies of *Alice's Adventures in Wonderland*.

What to do

- To revise tenses, go around the class asking volunteers to say simple sentences in the past, present or future. If the class is familiar, use specific tense names including simple, continuous/progressive or perfect. Write some of their examples on the board to revise tense formation. Then focus on the perfect tenses with the 'have/had' auxiliary and the past participle. Point out how auxiliary verbs agree with the subject in the perfect: I/you/we/they *have* and he/she/it *has*.

- Discuss how to show time relationships in sentences, particularly in third person narratives. Write on the board: Alice says she has learned her lesson. Alice said she had learned her lesson. Ask: *Why is it 'had' (past perfect) not 'has' (present perfect) in the second sentence?* (It shows learning the lesson happened before Alice said it: *learn* must be further back in the past than *says/said*.) Demonstrate the relationships by drawing a timeline labelled 'Past Present Future' and place the action in each sentence on the timeline.

- Organise the class in pairs to invent sentences practising different time relationships by completing sentence starters (for example, 'she said/says…', 'he thought/thinks…') using the correct perfect tense. Share their sentences, using the timeline to check the order of events.

Differentiation
Support: Give children sentence starter cards to sort into present and past tense (says/said, thinks/thought and so on). They can finish each sentence or match them to sentence end cards you provide.

Extension: Ask pairs to explore the relationship between the future perfect and present tenses, for example: 'Before Alice goes to sleep, she will have grown again.'

5. Tell me more

Objective
To use expanded noun phrases.
What you need
Notebooks.

What to do

- Write 'Alice' in the middle of the board and ask the class for adjectives to describe her, encouraging interesting ones. Use their suggestions to create a mind map surrounding Alice, noting whether the adjectives describe her physical appearance or her personality.

- Invite a volunteer to complete a sentence 'Alice is a…girl', using two or more of the adjectives. Revise commas separating adjectives in a list with 'and' between the last two. Explain that the adjectives work together in a phrase to modify or tell us more in a neat, concise way about the noun 'girl'.

- Now add phrases onto the mind map, for example 'with long, blond hair' and invite further suggestions from the class. Demonstrate how to combine more than one noun phrase: 'the thoughtful and considerate, little girl with a blue dress', adding adjectives and phrases both before and after the noun. Encourage inventive suggestions from the class to add to the mind map.

- Organise the class into small groups, first to invent expanded noun phrases for one or more character from *Alice's Adventures in Wonderland* and then to use them in sentences in their notebooks. Remind them that more than one noun in a sentence can be modified by a noun phrase. Share their ideas in a plenary session.

Differentiation
Support: Give children a wordbank to choose adjectives from.

Extension: Ask groups to rewrite their sentences using different adjectives to create a different mood or atmosphere.

6. Consistency matters

Objective
To use bullet points, punctuating them consistently.
What you need
Copies of *Alice's Adventures in Wonderland*, notebooks, photocopiable page 24 'Keeping consistent'.

What to do

- Revise list writing with the class. Write on the board: 'Alice saw cupboards shelves maps pictures and a jar of marmalade'. Invite a volunteer to add the correct punctuation. While a comma before 'and' is not incorrect, it is usual to have 'and' alone, consistency being the important thing.

- Ask: *How else could the list have been written?* (one under the other) Re-organise the sentence as a bulleted list following the stem, *'Alice saw'*. Ask: *What punctuation mark should introduce the list?* (colon – colons introduce: a list, dialogue, idea) Add the colon. Ask: *Should each list item start with a capital letter? Why?* (no; each item continues the sentence) Ask: *When would the list items begin with a capital?* (if each bullet is a sentence or the introduction is not a stem)

- Discuss whether each bullet should end with a comma or a semi-colon, according to your teaching policy, and whether the list should end with a full stop. Bring the discussion round to emphasise that while there are no hard and fast rules, bullets must be consistent – not just in punctuation but also how they start and whether each is a full sentence. Demonstrate the punctuation possibilities on the board.

- Hand out photocopiable page 24 'Keeping consistent' for individuals to complete. Review their answers as a class, encouraging discussion of different possibilities.

Differentiation
Support: Allow children to complete the first half only or to work in pairs.

Extension: Ask them to make lists of characters Alice likes and dislikes, giving each an appropriate introduction.

Active or passive?

- Rewrite each verb in the passive voice.

They clean _____

The card hides _____

She gave _____

Alice will tell _____

- Identify whether each sentence is active or passive, and then rewrite them in the opposite voice.

1. The gardeners planted a white rose by mistake.

_____

_____

_____

2. An announcement will be made by the King.

_____

_____

_____

3. She tucks the flamingo neatly under her arm.

_____

_____

4. The letter that was written by the prisoner was read by Bill.

_____

_____

_____

- Choose a suitable subject and rewrite the sentence below in the active voice.
The Cheshire-Cat was summoned and ordered to kiss the Queen's hand.

_____

_____

_____

Silent-letter croquet

- Take turns rolling the dice and moving your counters towards the finishing post.

- If you land on a flamingo, go to the next hoop. To get through a hoop, write two words that contain the hoop's silent letter. You can't use a word that's been used before!

30	31 N	32	33	FINISH
29 T	28	27	26	25 H
20	21	22 G	23	24
19	18 W	17	16 P	15
10	11	12 P	13	14
9 B	8	7	6	5 U
START	1	2 K	3	4

Keeping consistent

- Correct the two lists so they are written and punctuated consistently.

1. Queen of Hearts croquet equipment includes
- Flamingos
- hedgehogs,
- Cards

2. Alice wanted to:
- grow much smaller
- use the golden key, and
- opening the tiny door
- Then, enter the garden

- Complete a list of things you think Alice learned about Wonderland, using consistent punctuation and format.

Alice learned the following things about Wonderland:

- Read Extract 4 and summarise it using bullet points. Use only relevant information.

In Victorian times, life for children was very different to today:

PLOT, CHARACTER & SETTING ▶

1. A Wonderlandscape

Objective
To increase their familiarity with a wide range of books.

What you need
Copies of *Alice's Adventures in Wonderland*, photocopiable page 29 'Wonderland cards', large coloured card.

What to do
- Talk about the book being a fantasy novel. Ask: *What fantasy novels do you know?* (Harry Potter series, Philip Pullman novels, Narnia series) *What identifies them as fantasy novels?* (mainly characters and settings) Initiate a discussion on the key features of fantasy novels, using questions such as: *Is it enough for the setting to be not real?* (no – not if it is 'true-to-life') *What is fantasy rather than just unreal?* (strange or impossible landscapes, characters or events, magical powers, and so on)

- Organise the children into groups to analyse *Alice's Adventures in Wonderland* and its characters and why it's considered a fantasy novel. Explain that they should first brainstorm the main characters and settings, then share them out among the group to complete cards from photocopiable page 29 'Wonderland cards'. Once their cards are done, they can create a 'Wonderlandscape' on large coloured card, together with illustrations showing which characters belong in which setting.

Differentiation
Support: Organise the children into mixed ability groups.

Extension: Encourage children to research 'anthropomorphism' and identify which characters fall into this category.

2. Getting to know Alice

Objective
To draw inferences about characters.

What you need
Copies of *Alice's Adventures in Wonderland*, photocopiable page 30 'Evidence'.

What to do
- Ask: *How old is Alice?* If the children begin guessing, ask: *How do you know?* (her age is not given) Then ask: *How old do you think Alice is? Why?* Encourage suggestions backed by textual evidence and show the difference from guessing – there may be no 'right' answer, but suggestions must be based on the text.

- Now draw up a list together of what they know about Alice by the end of Chapter 1: who she is, what she thinks and likes, why she does things and so on. Write their suggestions on the board, differentiating between fact and inference: for example, Alice has an older sister (fact), Alice enjoys making daisy chains (inference from 'whether the pleasure of making a daisy chain…') to demonstrate how inferences are supported by textual evidence.

- Organise the class into groups and hand out photocopiable page 30 'Evidence'. Decide whether the children complete the sheet based on a chapter, or on what they know so far; they can add to it as they read the book. Share their ideas in a plenary at the end.

Differentiation
Support: Work through a section of a chapter with selected groups to identify evidence, asking whether it's factual or what inference it leads to.

Extension: Children can complete an evidence sheet for another character.

3. Identifying themes

Objective

To identify and discuss a theme.

What you need

Copies of *Alice's Adventures in Wonderland*.

What to do

- Ask: *What's the difference between the main idea and a theme of a story?* (Main idea: what happens in the plot; theme: a message that can be learned from the story or a 'big idea' running through the story.) To ensure the children understand the difference, summarise a short story or fable, such as 'The Tortoise and the Hare' (a tortoise and a hare have a race to see who is the fastest), then invite a volunteer to identify the theme/message. Discuss how the message isn't stated but has to be inferred from clues or events in the plot. Being initially to entertain the Liddell girls, the story wasn't necessarily intended to convey a moral or make serious observations. Despite this, various themes can be identified; the important thing is to build the children's confidence at identifying and discussing themes.

- Write 'Personal identity' on the board and ask the children to scan Chapter 1 for examples relating to this theme (do cats eat bats or vice-versa? being the 'right' size – for the door; what it would be like to shrink and 'shut out like a candle'; Alice pretending to be two people, and so on).

- Now ask them to find examples demonstrating the same theme in Chapter 2. Bring the class together for a plenary and discuss their findings and what general observations, if any, can be inferred.

Differentiation

Support: Work through Chapter 2 with groups to identify relevant examples.

Extension: Ask children to explore the book for further examples relating to this theme to share with the class, for example, Chapters 5 and 6.

4. Asking questions

Objective

To ask questions to demonstrate their understanding and answer questions using evidence from the text.

What you need

Copies of *Alice's Adventures in Wonderland*.

What to do

- Begin by asking: *What's your favourite scene or chapter in the story? Why?* Model the sort of answer you want by telling them your favourite scene and why, reading out specific extracts to illustrate your view. Invite volunteers to give their favourites, encouraging them to read back from the text.

- Choose one of the suggestions and ask a few questions, focusing on their comprehension of the text and language in relation to plot, characters and setting. Demonstrate the difference between questions directly answerable from the text (lower order): *What was the caterpillar doing when Alice first saw him?* (smoking a hookah) or *What does 'languid' mean?* (moving or speaking slowly and with little energy), and higher order ones requiring more inference: *Why does Alice feel she isn't 'herself'?* (feels changed by being different sizes and unable to remember what she used to) *Why does the caterpillar put Alice out of temper?* (short answers and constant contradictions) *Has Alice really changed?* (own suggestions)

- Once the children are comfortable with the different types of questions and answers, organise them into pairs to come up with ten questions (and answers) based on a chapter/scene (they choose or you designate). Encourage a range of lower and higher order questions. After an allocated time, they can ask another pair their questions and compare answers.

Differentiation

Support: Children can come up with fewer questions/answers or just lower order ones.

Extension: Encourage the children to focus on higher order questions and answers.

5. Tell me the truth

Objective
To distinguish between statements of fact and opinion.

What you need
Copies of *Alice's Adventures in Wonderland*, notebooks.

What to do

- Begin by asking the class the difference between fact and opinion, inviting examples of each. Together build up shared definitions: fact – something known to be true or that can be shown to have happened or existed, for example: Alice is a girl; opinion – personal view or judgement: Alice is easily annoyed. Explain that opinions can be based on feelings as well as facts, for example, 'I think the Queen of Hearts is bloodthirsty', although they should be backed by reasons from the text and personal experience, for example, '...because she wants to chop off everyone's head and ordinary people don't do that'.

- Read Chapter 5 until Alice starts reciting 'You are old, Father William'. Ask: *What was the caterpillar's first question?* (Who are you?) Then ask: *What factual answers could Alice have given?* (girl, age, name, where she lives and so on) *What 'opinion' answers could Alice have given?* Prompt the class with examples, such as 'I am a polite person'. Have a discussion on whether facts or opinions tell you more about a person or character.

- Organise the class into pairs and allocate a character to each. Explain that they must research the character and write five factual things and then their opinion (backed by reasons) of the character in their notebooks. Share and evaluate their findings in a plenary session.

Differentiation
Support: Allow children to list fewer facts.

Extension: Children can complete the activity for other characters of their choice.

6. A dry race

Objective
To identify how language and presentation contribute to meaning.

What you need
Copies of *Alice's Adventures in Wonderland*, dictionaries.

What to do

- Organise the children into groups to read Chapter 3 aloud, with one narrator and the others as characters: Lory, Alice, Mouse, Duck, Dodo, Crab and young Crab, Magpie and Canary. Encourage them to skim over their parts first to help them enjoy the dialogue and appreciate the absurdity of the scene during the reading – decide whether there's time to act it out as well.

- After reading, ask the children to look up 'caucus' in a dictionary (a campaign race to lead a political party or group). Ask a volunteer to explain why the 'caucus race' is humorous in this chapter (the motley group run an actual race, without criteria for winning, so everyone wins). Now ask: *What other wordplay is in the chapter title?* (Tale: the mouse's *tale* later in the chapter is shaped as a *tail*) and then: *Which dictionary meaning of 'dry' explains the humour in the Mouse's 'dry' speech?*

- Explain that in their groups, first, the children must identify other wordplay and humour in the chapter – for example, in word meanings, language, illustrations, or events. Encourage them to use dictionaries to look up unfamiliar words. Then, they should choose two or three interesting adjectives to depict the different characters based on how they are portrayed in the text.

- Come back together at the end to share ideas and discuss the different characters.

Differentiation
Support: Provide an adjective bank to choose from to describe the characters.

Extension: Ask children to write a set of rules for 'How to run a caucus race' using numbered steps and command verbs.

7. When I woke up

Objective
To identify how...structure...contributes to meaning.

What you need
Copies of *Alice's Adventures in Wonderland*, notebooks.

What to do

• Revise classic story structure on the board. Mark out a timeline of standard plot development: initial situation, conflict/problem, build-up, climax and resolution, conclusion. Hold a general story structure discussion and invite volunteers to relate this structure to a book they have read recently and decide whether it follows the model.

• Together, analyse the structure of *Alice's Adventures in Wonderland*. Use questions to prompt discussion and invite volunteers to annotate your timeline with plot events. Ask: *How does the story begin?* (Alice is bored and follows a white rabbit down a hole.) *What was the main conflict/problem?* (Alice wants to reach the garden but is the wrong size.) *What happens along the way?* (various) *What were the climax and resolution?* (court scene; Alice reaches correct size and acknowledges they are just cards) Ask: *How does it end?* (Alice wakes and it was all a dream.)

• Ask: *What do you think of stories ending with 'it was all a dream'?* After a brief discussion, explain this is often a poor ending because no proper resolution/conclusion is necessarily developed. Ask: *Do you think the 'all a dream' ending works in Alice's Adventures in Wonderland? Why?* (Encourage reflective answers.) Then organise the class to brainstorm in pairs for a different ending where it's not 'all a dream'. Share their ideas at the end.

Differentiation
Support: Allow children to work in groups you can oversee and guide.

Extension: Ask children to write out their new ending in their notebooks.

8. Navigating Wonderland

Objectives
To distinguish between fact and opinion and provide reasons for their views.

What you need
Copies of *Alice's Adventures in Wonderland*, photocopiable page 31 'Caterpillars and Mushrooms', slips of playing-card-sized paper, dice.

What to do

• Begin with a quick quiz on Chapter 1. First, ask two questions requiring an answer from the text or illustrations, for example: *What was the White Rabbit wearing when Alice first saw him?* (jacket/coat, shirt, cravat and waistcoat) *Why did Alice drink from the bottle labelled 'DRINK ME'?* (because it was not marked 'poison'.) Then, ask two questions that ask for a personal opinion or reflection backed by reasons, for example: *Would you have drunk from the bottle labelled 'DRINK ME'?* (Demonstrate that these questions require a 'because' answer: I would/wouldn't have drunk from the bottle because…)

• Organise the class into groups of three or four. Hand out copies of photocopiable page 31 'Caterpillars and Mushrooms' and a pile of card-sized slips of blank paper. Allocate each group a chapter or chapters of the book and explain that they must make ten game cards based on their allocated chapter: five 'question' cards that can be answered from the text or illustrations, with the answer written below, and five 'because' cards with questions asking for opinion-based answers with reasons. Once the cards are made (labelled 'question' or 'because' on the blank side), mix them up and distribute them between groups to play the game.

• This activity can be adapted for a single chapter or section, or to have a specific focus of your choice by writing your own question cards.

Differentiation
Support and extension: Ensure that groups are of mixed-ability.

Wonderland cards

- Cut out the Wonderland cards and complete them.

Character:

_____

animal ☐   person ☐   other ☐

Physical characteristics:

_____

_____

Fantastical characteristics/actions:

_____

_____

Character:

_____

animal ☐   person ☐   other ☐

Physical characteristics:

_____

_____

Fantastical characteristics/actions:

_____

_____

Setting:

_____

What it looks like:

_____

_____

Fantastical elements:

_____

_____

Setting:

_____

What it looks like:

_____

_____

Fantastical elements:

_____

_____

Evidence

- Fill in the table to develop your ideas about a character.

Character name _____

Character trait	Evidence in text				Fact or inference?

Caterpillars and Mushrooms

- Throw the dice to move through Wonderland. If you land on a caterpillar, answer a 'question' card. If you land on a mushroom, answer a 'because' card.
- If you land on a Queen or can't answer a card, miss a turn!

TALK ABOUT IT ▶

1. Who are you?

Objective
To speak audibly and fluently.

What you need
Copies of *Alice's Adventures in Wonderland*, notebooks, photocopiable page 35 'Introduce yourself'.

Cross-curricular link
PSHE

What to do

- Ask the children to name some characters Alice meets in Wonderland. Together, skim the book for the parts where Alice meets a character for the first time. Ask: *Does she introduce herself to each character? Is she polite? How do the conversations start? What challenges does she face?* (language, her size, rude/chaotic behaviour, disinterest)

- Ask: *Do you like meeting new people or introducing yourself to others?* Share personal experiences like meeting your new teacher, a relative or a new pupil at school. Discuss some of the challenges they might have, like feeling shy or embarrassed, meeting someone from a different culture or language group or disliking the person.

- Talk about how to introduce yourself formally in a group. Include appropriate body language, voice projection and things you might say. Let them fill in photocopiable page 35 'Introduce yourself' to make notes and prepare themselves. In groups, let them take turns introducing themselves. Once everyone has had a turn, let them repeat the main facts of the person sitting next to them – to check if they were listening.

Differentiation
Support: Change groups to pairs if anyone would rather not face a group.

Extension: The children can introduce a character in role to the whole class.

2. Rhymes and nonsense

Objective
To prepare poems to read aloud and perform.

What you need
Copies of *Alice's Adventures in Wonderland*, enlarged copies of the rhymes from the story.

What to do

- Remind the children that the author loved wordplay and experimenting with words. He believed that you could combine order and nonsense, which is evident in many of his poems and rhymes. Most of his poems are parodies (comical imitations) of well-known poems and rhymes of the time. Children found it very funny because it made fun of all the well-known poems they knew.

- Ask: *What does choral verse mean?* (A group narrates a poem, using various vocal combinations and expressions to bring out the meaning, tone and structure.) Explain that they are going to perform a fun choral verse.

- Working in groups of four or five, let the children choose one of the nonsense poems from the text. First, they should practise reading the poem aloud, then encourage them to experiment – trying out different voices and expressions for different parts of the poem, reading some parts together or using actions as well. Provide enlarged copies of the poems for them to annotate.

- Let the groups perform their poems to the class.

Differentiation
Support: Support less-confident performers by showing that they don't have to perform any parts on their own.

Extension: Perform to another audience. Let the children dress in character.

3. In the hot seat

Objective

To gain, maintain and monitor the interest of the listener.

What you need

Copies of *Alice's Adventures in Wonderland*, photocopiable page 36 'Rule check'.

Cross-curricular link

PSHE

What to do

- Turn to Chapter 8 and read together from '"Get to your places!" shouted the Queen...' to the chapter end. Ask: *What is croquet?* (It is a game played by two or four players: players must hit a ball through six hoops in the correct sequence and in each direction. The side that completes the course first wins.) *Has anyone in the class played it?* (Discuss their experiences.)

- Ask: *What problems does Alice experience when she tries to play the game?* (people running in all directions; the ground wasn't flat; the balls were hedgehogs that kept crawling away; the mallets were live flamingos that kept turning around; the hoops were doubled-up card soldiers who kept walking around; no one waited for their turn; they were arguing; the Queen was shouting; not playing fairly; no rules) *What structures were missing?* (order; correct sequence; rules; a referee; correct equipment and surface area) Ask: *Why do games have rules?* (so everyone knows what to do)

- Divide the children into small groups. Hand out photocopiable page 36 'Rule check' and let them discuss and note down the rules and structures required in each situation. If they don't know all the rules they can invent sensible ones.

- Allow time for groups to report back to the class.

Differentiation

Extension: Children invent rules for some of the scenes in the book, for example, falling down a rabbit-hole; growing and shrinking; a mad tea party, and working on the Queen's garden.

4. What a story!

Objective

To participate in debates.

What you need

Copies of *Alice's Adventures in Wonderland*, notebooks.

What to do

- Authority and punishment are themes in the story. Ask: *Why do you think these themes were used in a children's fantasy novel?* (The story was written in Victorian times. Alice is a little girl who stands up to authority and exposes the ridiculousness of the punishment handed out to anyone who does the same.)

- Have a discussion about punishment in Victorian times. Ask: *What were people punished for? Did the punishment always fit the crime? How were children punished at school? Compare punishment then and now. Has it changed?*

- Divide the class into four groups and explain that they will debate the topic 'Children should not be punished'. Two groups will argue for the topic and two groups will argue against it.

- In their groups, let them brainstorm the topic and come up with at least five good points to support their argument. They should choose a representative to present their argument to the other side.

- Organise the classroom so that the representatives face the rest of the class. Give each a chance to present their argument. Allow time at the end for questions from the floor. The audience should take notes while listening to the debate.

- Let the class vote on who they think had the best argument.

Differentiation

Support: In small groups, children offer their ideas and opinions on the topic.

Extension: Children research the rules of debating and conduct a formal debate on another issue related to the book, or an issue related to school.

5. Act it out

Objective

To participate in performances.

What you need

Copies of *Alice's Adventures in Wonderland*, space for groups to practise and present.

What to do

• Alice's experiences in Wonderland are dreamlike and rather bizarre. Ask: *What other words would you use to describe them?* (absurd, strange, foolish, crazy, illogical, ludicrous, nonsensical, ridiculous) The humour in the story is something that grows on you the more familiar you become with the story and its context. One way to become familiar with the text is to act it out.

• Choose readers to represent different characters and read together three scenes from the story, for example, Chapter 7 'A Mad Tea-Party', Chapter 8 'The Queen's Croquet-Ground' or Chapter 11 'Who Stole the Tarts?' Ask: *Which characters are involved in each scene? Who speaks? What is the setting?*

• Explain they will be acting out these scenes. Discuss the roles and responsibilities to ensure this activity is successful. Allocate the following roles and responsibilities: a producer, co-producer, props, time manager and so on.

• Organise the children into groups according to the characters required in each scene. Ensure groups have an even spread of confident and less-confident speakers. Let them decide who plays which character and who has a speaking/non-speaking part (even shy or quiet children may enjoy the opportunity to act a speaking part).

• Give them a set time to plan and practise their scene. Then present to the class.

Differentiation

Support: Choose a dialogue from the story to enact.

Extension: Children can act out their scene for a younger class, giving an introduction to it first.

6. A different perspective

Objective

To consider and evaluate different viewpoints, attending to and building on the contributions of others.

What you need

Copies of *Alice's Adventures in Wonderland*, photocopiable page 37 'What's your view?'

What to do

• In the story, Alice's size keeps changing. Ask: *Why do you think the author made size an important element in the story?* (The story was written for children. As a little girl, Alice is aware of growing and changing size. Her experiences, emotions and attitudes differ according to her size.) *How does Alice feel when she is small? What things can and can't she do? When she is big how does it affect her ability to get on with the other characters?* (Invite discussion.) Consider the final scene. Ask: *What size does Alice become? How does this affect her attitude?* (She returns to her full size and stands up to the Queen and speaks her mind.)

• Using photocopiable page 37 'What's your view?', discuss the different words we use to describe 'small' and 'big'. Ask: *If you could be 10 inches small (about 25 cm) or 9 feet tall (about 2.7 metres), what would you choose? Why?*

• In small groups the children can then use the photocopiable page 37 'What's your view?' to guide a discussion on things you can/can't do according to your size. The guided discussion will encourage the children to see things from a different perspective. Afterwards, let them report back to the class.

Differentiation

Support: Monitor the group discussions.

Extension: The children can draw a timeline of their life showing when they were able to do different things according to their age, size and maturity.

Introduce yourself

- Use the mind map to plan how to introduce yourself.
- Write your name in the star in the middle. Choose six headings from the list in the box and write each one in a circle.
- Make notes under each heading.

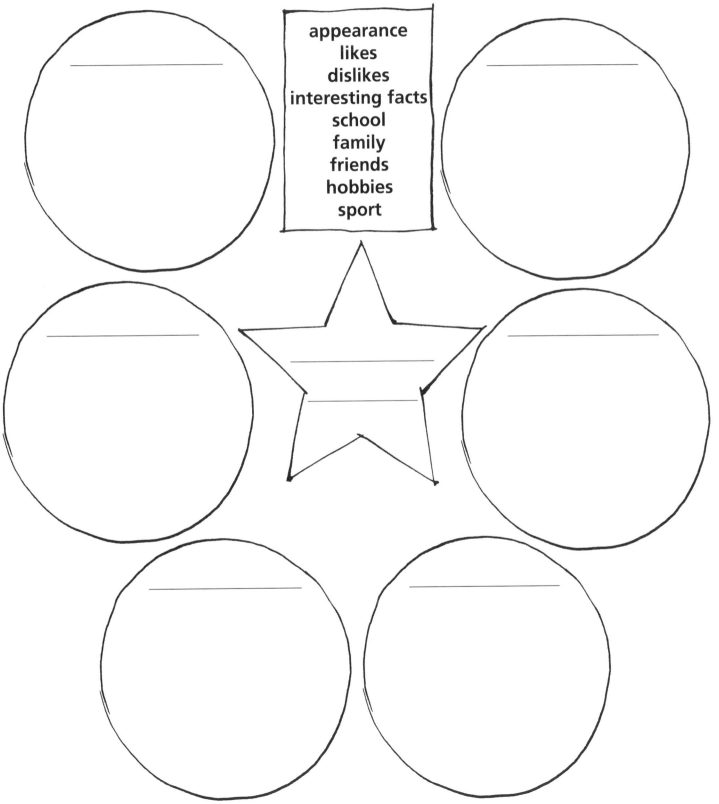

appearance
likes
dislikes
interesting facts
school
family
friends
hobbies
sport

Rule check

- Discuss some sensible rules for each of the following scenarios.
- Write down the most important rules.

Your favourite card or board game

Your favourite playground game

Meeting a stranger

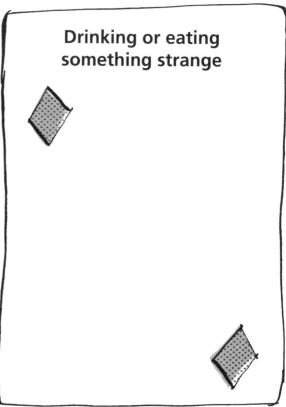

Drinking or eating something strange

What's your view?

● Discuss the following questions with your group or a partner and make notes.

Think of **four** synonyms for the word 'small'. Order them from smallest to biggest.

| 1. | 2. | 3. | 4. |

Think of **four** synonyms for the word 'big'. Order them from smallest to biggest.

| 1. | 2. | 3. | 4. |

If you could drink a potion and become 25 centimetres small, list the things you would struggle to do at home. Think of advantages and disadvantages. If you have a pet, how would your feelings towards it change?

_____

_____

_____

_____

_____

If you could drink a potion and become 3 metres tall, list the challenges you would encounter at school.
Ask yourself questions like: Where would you sit?
What games could you play or not play?
Would your friends still want you around?

_____

_____

_____

_____

_____

GET WRITING ▶

1. Proverbial proverbs

Objective

To propose changes to grammar/sentence structure to clarify meaning.

What you need

Copies of *Alice's Adventures in Wonderland*, photocopiable page 41 'Sensible proverbs'.

What to do

- Read the dialogues with the Duchess in Chapters 6 and 9. Ask: *What do you notice about how the Duchess speaks?* (Accept various answers but guide the children to identifying her poor use of proverbs and sayings.) Ask: *What is a proverb?* (an old, popular saying that is used in a particular context to present some general truth or moral) Proverbs and similar literature were popular at the time of *Alice's Adventures in Wonderland*.

- Help the children to identify the proverbs that the Duchess uses and decide if her wording and/or use of the proverb is correct. (Correct wording: grinning like a Cheshire cat; mind your own business; love makes the world go round; take care of the pennies and the pounds will take care of themselves; birds of a feather flock together; nothing is what it seems; pigs might fly). Discuss the effect of the incorrect wording. (It creates humour, especially to readers at the time who knew their proverbs well!) Ask: *Can you spot the saying that the author made up?* (The more there is of mine, the less there is of yours.)

- Hand out photocopiable page 41 'Sensible proverbs'. Ask pairs to unjumble the proverbs and attempt to explain them. Discuss their answers.

Differentiation

Extension: Research the meaning, origin and context of other old proverbs from Victorian times.

2. Reviewing books

Objective

To identify the purpose of the writing and select the appropriate form.

What you need

Copies of *Alice's Adventures in Wonderland*, photocopiable page 42 'Book review', access to the Internet for further research.

What to do

- Read the first page of *Alice's Adventures in Wonderland*. Ask: *Why was Alice bored?* (She had nothing to do.) *Why wasn't she interested in her sister's book?* (It had no pictures or conversations.) Ask: *What type of book do you think it was?*

- Ask: *What type of books do you prefer: picture books, fiction books with/without pictures, non-fiction books? Why?* (Encourage individual answers. Discuss the pros and cons of pictures in books. Compare fiction and non-fiction books.)

- Look at the *Alice* cover. Ask: *Is there a picture? What does it show? Are there pictures inside?*

- Ask the children to skim through *Alice* and look at all the pictures. The pictures were drawn by a famous cartoonist at the time – John Tenniel. Lewis Carroll chose him for his style. Ask: *Do you like the pictures? Do they help you understand the story? Do the pictures describe things as you imagined?* (Encourage individual answers.)

- Ask the children to choose a children's fiction book they've enjoyed (with pictures) and write a review using photocopiable page 42 'Book review'.

Differentiation

Support: Children can write a review of *Alice's Adventures in Wonderland*.

Extension: Let the children design their own book review page.

3. What is weird?

Objective
To describe and compare characters, integrating dialogue to convey character.

What you need
Copies of *Alice's Adventures in Wonderland*.

What to do

- Write two headings on the board: 'weird' and 'normal' Ask: *Do you think the characters in Wonderland are weird or normal?* (weird) *Why are they so weird?* (Wonderland is a dream world where people and animals do not act 'normally'.) Invite synonyms for 'weird' to enhance their understanding of the word. Remind the children that in the Victorian era there were strict rules about behaviour – what was acceptable and what was not.

- Let the children work in pairs to skim through the story to identify weird characters and scenes in Wonderland. They should note the things that make them seem weird: the setting, what they say, how they look, how they speak. Then, note the 'normal' behaviour one would expect. Ask: *How would you expect a duchess, queen, cook or gardener to behave? How do animals behave normally?* Come together and discuss their findings. Write notes on the board under the headings. Ask: *Who seems to be the most 'normal' character in Wonderland?* (Alice) Then list in order down to the weirdest.

- Working on their own, children should choose two characters from the book and write a paragraph describing them from Alice's point of view. The paragraph can begin: 'Today I met a...' They should write in the first person, imagining and expressing Alice's thoughts and giving examples of the weird behaviour and conversations she encounters.

Differentiation

Support: The children can describe meeting only one weird character from the story.

Extension: Encourage children to describe characters through their actions and dialogue, using their own words to describe them.

4. A new chapter...

Objectives
To consider how authors have developed characters and settings in narratives; to proofread for spelling and punctuation errors.

What you need
Copies of *Alice's Adventures in Wonderland*.

What to do

- Lewis Carroll apparently wrote some of the chapters after the story was completed. Ask the children to guess which chapters they might have been (invite ideas). Ask: *Why do you think it was possible for Lewis Carroll to include new chapters after completing the story?* (The story does not have a conventional plot with a beginning, middle and end. Chapters are mostly self-contained.)

- Ask the children to imagine creating a new character (or characters) for Wonderland and brainstorm ideas. Let them draw a picture of the new character and list adjectives to describe what the character is like. Then let them describe their new character to a partner. Share and develop ideas together.

- Tell the children they are going to plan the start of a new chapter. They need to think of a title and an opening paragraph where Alice meets the new character/s. They should describe the setting – somewhere in Wonderland – and write a short dialogue between the two characters.

- The children should review and edit their work, checking for errors and refining vocabulary, especially expressive verbs to replace 'said'. Remind them to check their speech punctuation using the book.

- Let them read their chapter starters to the class. The class could then decide which chapter starter they think fits best with the story.

Differentiation

Support: Focus on writing a new dialogue between two characters (existing characters or new ones).

Extension: Include a short nonsense rhyme to go into the chapter starter.

5. Make it clear

Objective

To use organisational and presentational devices to structure text and to guide the reader.

What you need

Copies of *Alice's Adventures in Wonderland*, photocopiable page 43 'Begin at the beginning'.

What to do

- There seems to be little order in Wonderland and a lot of confusion. Refer to various scenes in the book where Alice finds herself confused about a procedure or activity. Read Chapter 3 from '"What *is* a Caucus-race?" said Alice...', Chapter 8 from 'Alice thought she had never seen such a curious croquet ground in all her life...' and Chapter 10 from '"What sort of a dance is it?"...' Have a class discussion giving reasons why there is such confusion. The children should identify the lack of clear instructions.

- Using photocopiable page 43 'Begin at the beginning', the children should work in pairs to unjumble the order of the instructions to make comfits. Remind them to look for clues like headings and key conjunctions like 'next' and 'finally'.

- Ask volunteers to share their answers. Ask: *Do these instructions make sense once they're in the correct order?* (yes)

- Ask the children to choose a game or activity from *Alice's Adventures in Wonderland* (croquet, a game of cards, holding a meeting, changing size, mock turtle soup) and write out the instructions. They should include headings and key words that indicate the order. They can also include a simple diagram with labels.

Differentiation

Support: The children can demonstrate a simple classroom activity like 'How to sharpen your pencil' before writing down the instructions.

Extension: Children choose their own topic and write a set of numbered instructions.

6. Becoming authors

Objective

To identify the audience for and purpose of the writing, selecting appropriate form and using other similar writing as models.

What you need

Copies of *Alice's Adventures in Wonderland*, Internet access for research.

What to do

- In Chapter 7, Alice meets the Hatter, sometimes called the Mad Hatter. He asks Alice a riddle, 'Why is a raven like a writing-desk?', but Alice doesn't know the answer. Ask: *Can you think of an answer to the riddle?* (Lewis Carroll didn't actually write it with an answer in mind. Later answers include: they both flap open and closed; they both produce notes; they both have quills!)

- Lewis Carroll was a word puzzle master. Riddles are a type of word puzzle. They require a good understanding of language and a good general knowledge. One of the oldest known riddles comes from the ancient civilisation of Sumer: 'There is a house. One enters it blind and comes out seeing. What is it?' (a school) Some riddles rhyme, like this one from *The Hobbit*: 'Voiceless it cries, wingless flutters, toothless bites, mouthless mutters.' The answer is 'the wind'.

- Let the children research riddles and bring them to share with the class. Based on the many riddles available, they should then write their own riddles – with or without a rhyming pattern.

Differentiation

Support: Give the children a specific structure and topic. Include information about the topic so they have some facts to include in the riddle. They can work with a partner.

Extension: Encourage children to write longer riddles with a rhyming pattern and increased vocabulary. Refer to examples like the one in *Harry Potter and the Goblet of Fire* or Old English/Viking riddles.

Sensible proverbs

- Unjumble these old proverbs and write them out correctly in the 'Make sense' column.
- Explain their meaning *or* use them in context in the 'Make meaning' column.

Stuff and nonsense	Make sense	Make meaning
your hatch don't they count before chickens		

Stuff and nonsense	Make sense	Make meaning
no milk use over crying spilt it's		

Stuff and nonsense	Make sense	Make meaning
the cooks many broth spoil too		

Stuff and nonsense	Make sense	Make meaning
throw with water out don't baby the bath the		

Stuff and nonsense	Make sense	Make meaning
while is strike iron hot the		

Book review

● Write a review of one of your favourite children's fiction books.

What is the title?

_____

_____

What is the genre?

_____

_____

Who is the author?
Give some background.

_____

_____

_____

Who is the illustrator?
Give some background.

_____

_____

Who are the main
characters in the story?

● _____

● _____

● _____

● _____

● _____

● _____

● _____

Do you like the style of the pictures?
Why/Why not?

_____

_____

Describe the setting and plot.

_____

_____

_____

_____

_____

_____

Who is your favourite character?
Why?

_____

_____

_____

_____

Who is your least favourite
character? Why?

_____

_____

_____

_____

Begin at the beginning

● Using the following writing frame, unjumble the instructions below.

Method: Allow the mixture to cool then repeat by adding more syrup until the comfits are well-coated. Heat the syrup to about 235°F until it reaches the soft-ball stage. Next, put $\frac{1}{3}$ cup of seeds into a metal bowl with high sides. Maintain this temperature by reducing the heat slightly. Quickly mix it with a fork in a circular motion until the clump of seeds dries and the seeds separate. After 5–10 coats, allow to dry overnight in an open bowl. Use the ladle to spoon some syrup onto the seeds. First, make a sugar syrup by combining $\frac{1}{3}$ cup water with 1 cup sugar. **You need:** sugar, water, a thick-based pan, a metal bowl, seeds, a fork, a ladle.

How to make comfits:

You need:

_____

_____

_____

Method:

1. _____

_____

2. _____

_____

_____

3. _____

_____

4. _____

_____

5. _____

_____

6. _____

_____

7. _____

_____

8. _____

_____

ASSESSMENT ▶

1. Making sense of nonsense

Objectives

To understand what they read by drawing inferences; to check the book makes sense to them.

What you need

Copies of *Alice's Adventures in Wonderland*, photocopiable page 47 'No nonsense!'

What to do

- Explain to the children that they are going to complete a reading task that will check their understanding of a text. Revise and, if necessary, explain the different types and levels of questions: closed questions (require simple 'yes' or 'no' responses); open questions (require details); multiple choice questions (require you to choose an answer from ones provided); basic level questions (require you to find the answer directly from the text); middle level questions (require you to analyse information or classify); higher level questions (require you to interpret and apply the information – these can include visual literacy questions).

- Remind them that with any text, they should always begin by skimming and scanning it for clues and to get the context before reading the text in detail. Remind them to read the questions, and then re-read the text before attempting to write answers. Once they have followed these steps, they will be ready to begin. You can write these steps on the board for them to follow.

- Turn to Chapter 9 and hand out photocopiable page 47 'No nonsense!' Read through the chapter and questions together. Let them complete the questions individually.

2. Say what you mean

Objective

To participate actively in collaborative conversations and dialogues.

What you need

Copies of *Alice's Adventures in Wonderland*.

What to do

- Review some of the conversations in the book and analyse the characters through the dialogue. Ask: *From what the character says, what are they like and how do they feel?* Consider the conversation with the mouse in Chapter 1 and analyse the mouse's attitude and feelings towards Alice. Also, consider how Alice felt and why.

- When conversation is difficult, it is often helpful to have a third person to help communication. They ask both sides to explain how they feel and to have their say. Working in groups of three, the children should prepare and present an informal interview of two characters from the story. One of the children should be the interviewer or objective observer.

- Working together, the children should make a list of 'open' questions that will give the characters a chance to explain themselves to the others. Remind the children that 'open' questions encourage explanations and descriptions while 'closed' questions require a 'yes' or 'no' type answer. Once their list of questions is ready, the children should practise their interview in character. Finally, they can present their interviews to the class.

Differentiation

Support: Provide example questions such 'Why were you surprised to see her?' or 'Why didn't you offer her a seat?'

Extension: The children can turn their interview into a Q&A magazine article.

3. Alice dictionary

Objective

To use a dictionary to check spelling and meaning of words.

What you need

Copies of *Alice's Adventures in Wonderland*, dictionaries, coloured pencils, cardboard (optional).

What to do

- Alice is as a keen student who loves to use 'grand' words. Ask: *Why is some of the vocabulary she uses unfamiliar to children these days?* (The story was written in Victorian times, some of the vocabulary is 'old' and no longer in use.) Write the following words on the board: 'quarrelling', 'curtseying', 'knave', 'footman', 'simpleton'. Check if the children know what these words mean and challenge them to use the words in a sentence. Discuss any modern terms we use instead.

- Let the children sit in pairs and skim through the book, writing down any words that seem 'old' or unfamiliar. Come back together and invite ideas for the most difficult or uncommon words in the story. Write these on the board. Discuss their meanings.

- Hand out dictionaries. The children should work on their own to make their own picture dictionary of 'Alice words'. They can choose their own words from those discussed. Their dictionary should show the correct spelling, the word class, where applicable the singular and plural, a sentence with the word used in context and a simple picture. The children could use cardboard or plain white paper for display.

- Display their dictionary pages.

Differentiation

Support: Encourage the children to choose nouns as these are easier to explain and illustrate.

Extension: The children can learn the words for a spelling/vocabulary test.

4. Figuratively speaking

Objective

To discuss and evaluate how authors use language, including figurative language.

What you need

Copies of *Alice's Adventures in Wonderland*.

What to do

- Write the following sentences on the board: 'You are behaving like a clown.' 'The man was a clown, working in the circus.' Ask: *Which sentence is figurative?* (the first one) *Which sentence is literal?* (the second one) Discuss the difference between literal and figurative language. Literal language is straightforward, clear and means exactly what it says. Figurative language is descriptive and uses comparisons and wordplay to get a point across. Write the following terms on the board and ensure that the children understand their meaning: similes, metaphors, puns, personification, anthropomorphism, onomatopoeia, expressions/idiomatic sayings.

- Write the following examples on the board and ask the children to match them to one of the terms: 'Oh, how I wish I could shut up like a telescope!' (simile); '"Mine is a long and a sad tale!" said the Mouse.' (pun and anthropomorphism); 'no wise fish would go anywhere without a porpoise.' (pun); '"If you knew Time as well as I do," said the Hatter, "you wouldn't talk about wasting *it*. It's *him*."' (personification); '"Stuff and nonsense!" said Alice.' (expression); '"Hjckrrh!" from the Gryphon.' (onomatopoeia).

- In pairs, ask the children to scan the text for other examples of figurative language. They should write them out and describe the type of figurative language each one is.

Differentiation

Support: Provide more examples for the children to write out and explain.

Extension: Explain the effect of the figurative expressions in the context of the dialogue.

5. Calling all stage directors

Objective
To use organisational devices to structure text and to guide the reader.

What you need
An example of any playscript.

What to do

- Ask: *Who has been in a production and used a script?* (Invite responses.) If possible, show children an example of a script. Ask: *How is a script different from a book?* (The characters are listed at the beginning; there are scenes and acts, not chapters; stage notes/directions describe each scene – they are written in the present tense and may be in brackets or italics; no speech marks; character names are on the left side of the page with a colon after the name, and so on.)

- In pairs, let the children design their own checklist/ success criteria for how to write a playscript. They should use this checklist to guide their own writing. Discuss their checklists and agree to include the most important points.

- The children then continue working in pairs to plan, draft and write a rough draft for a scene from *Alice*. They should use the *Alice* text as inspiration, but they can also adapt the text to suit their play scene. Once they have a rough draft, they should use their checklist to edit and refine their work. You can use a similar checklist, agreed by the class, to assess their final product.

Differentiation

Support: Provide a playscript template to guide their writing.

Extension: Give each child a different scene to write (from the beginning of the story to the end) and then put it all together to form a complete play.

6. It was all a dream

Objectives
To write narratives, considering how authors develop characters and settings; to use the correct tense.

What you need
Copies of *Alice's Adventures in Wonderland*.

What to do

- The *Alice's Adventures in Wonderland* story has an unconventional plot. Despite this, there are certain formulae that the author uses to draw the reader in and lead us to a type of climax and ultimately the 'unpopular' story ending: she woke up and realised it was all a 'curious dream'.

- Write the following formula on the board: <u>Beginning</u>: The main character is bored – falls into a hole or goes through a mysterious doorway (falling asleep) – enters a strange land. <u>Middle:</u> She can't get to where she wants to go – encounters odd characters – has strange conversations – nobody can help her or understand her. <u>End:</u> She finds herself in a tight spot – she wakes up.

- With this basic formula, the children plan their own dream on a storyboard. Ask them to write the dream in the third person and in the past tense. They should describe the setting at the beginning of the story, and when the character enters the new world, giving the new world a name. They can invent some characters and at least two different scenes.

- Let the children prepare a rough draft and spend time editing before writing it out in neat. Ask the children to read their 'Wonderland' stories to the class.

Differentiation

Support: Let the children do this activity as a cartoon using frames to depict each scene.

Extension: Ask children to include dialogue in the story, and suggest including a nonsense rhyme or poem in the dream.